Two Suns in the Sky

Who Lives, Who Dies

Audiobook Transcript

Two Suns in the Sky

Who Lives, Who Dies

Audiobook Transcript

Your Own World Books
Nevada USA

KnowledgeMountain.org
TwoSunsinthesky.com
YowBooks.com
Kmmedia.org

Copyright

Two Suns in the Sky: Who Lives, Who Dies
Audiobook Transcript

First Edition – June 2017
Marshall Masters

Your Own World Books
An imprint of Knowledge Mountain Church
of Perpetual Genesis, NV, USA
knowledgemountain.org
twosunsinthesky.com
yowbooks.com
kmmedia.org

Trade Paperback
ISBN-13: 978-1546905455
ISBN-10: 1546905456

Notices

Trademarks

Table of Contents

Marshall's Motto

Destiny comes to those who listen,
and fate finds the rest.

So learn what you can learn,
do what you can do,
and never give up hope!

Purposeful Survival for an Enlightened Future

1

Introduction to Part 1

ANNOUNCER: Welcome to Two Suns in the Sky: Who Lives, Who Dies. To learn more about this three part audiobook series, visit twosunsinthesky.com. And now, part one, Purposeful Survival for an Enlightened Future with author and narrator, Marshall Masters.

Hello, I'm Marshall Masters, chief steward of the knowledge Mountain Church of Perpetual Genesis. Let's take a brief look ahead at what you'll learn in this three-part series.

In part one, were going to talk about purposeful survival for an enlightened future with a strategy we call enlightened continuity and comfort. The important thing to remember about this is that if you cannot afford bullets, beans, and bunkers, that's okay, because survival for you and your loved ones is really about becoming worth your weight in beans.

In part two Nibiru Pole Shift Who Lives and Who Dies, we'll address the difficult question of who lives and dies during the coming new Nibiru Pole Shift, one of several events, humanity must endure during this decade-long tribulation, which will claim thousands and millions of lives. However, the worst of all will be the pole shift for it will claim billions of lives. It occurs during the days of darkness when the Planet Nibiru passes between the orbits of Earth and Venus. Sadly only one in 10 will make it to what I call the backside a time when we see blue skies and taste sweet water once again.

Then in the third and final part of this series, the survival power of Perpetual Genesis, you'll learn about this, survival philosophy and why it is part of a larger toolkit, I've created through my experience as a Planet X researcher, author and publisher since 2002

To begin, let me briefly tell you about our church and then will examine the three leading causes of death during the Planet X tribulation.

2

About Knowledge Mountain Church of Perpetual Genesis

As a science driven researcher, I began to see the fatal flaws in conventional, me-and-mine survival strategies favored by many preppers over a decade ago. While the strategies come in many flavors all share the same Achilles heel, a shortsighted materialistic mindset within inevitable risk of hopelessness. The more I looked at these untested strategies for surviving the coming tribulation, the more I saw an urgent need to survive with hope for the future.

This is why I founded the knowledge Mountain Church of Perpetual Genesis in 2015. So what is Perpetual Genesis, let's imagine were writing an elevator together and you say to me Marshall you got 10 seconds to explain Perpetual Genesis to me. What would my answer be here is. Surviving the tribulation is not about holding onto things. It is about holding on to each other.

You may note that I use the term tribulation. And wonder if I'm talking about some kind of biblical judgment. I'm not in fact, we never use the word tribulation in any biblical or judgmental sense. Rather, we use it exactly as it is defined in the dictionary –

"A severe trial or suffering." This is a certainty, but that being said, while we do see a dark cloud coming, we choose to focus on the silver lining in that cloud and will discuss this in more depth later on in the series.

For now, suffice it to say that we believe the most precious gift God gives us is not life. This we give ourselves and our progeny. Rather, it is free will the energizing force of intention because it is through intention that universes are added to creation.

It is why we are born into this world to master our magnificent gift of free will, God always respects our right to choose, no differently than children taking their first steps, whether our steps are wise or unwise each choice is a learning step that will echo throughout eternity.

The one constant is that God always respects your paternal right to choose, so that you may gain mastery of your free will and thereby propel yourself forward along the path of ascension towards the light of God's love. Conversely each unwise decision is a step backwards away from the light of God's love.

On balance, the goal is to leave this world further along on the path of ascension than, when you entered it as this will determine the nature of your next incarnation. This is why the opportunity to judge yourself is God's gift to souls who incarnate.

That's it in a nutshell and why our church is about survival and not salvation. Salvation is for God and you to decide together without the meddling of others in your own way and in your own time. While we are always happy to explain our beliefs to others, we never proselytize.

As to your current faith, if you are happy with your core faith, then as the old saying goes, if it ain't broke, don't fix it. All we do is to fill in the gaps for those who cannot find the Planet X tribulation answers they seek, within the dogma, doctrine, checklists and mysticism of other faiths.

So what makes us different from other faiths we do not believe in pleading with God to work with us so that we can prevail as others around us suffer. Rather, we believe that God has a plan, and that as co-creators, we choose to pledge ourselves to God's plan. Therefore our message to God is simple. "We're in it with you!" This is what we call purposeful survival for an enlightened future.

We're not what is called a "big tent" church; rather, we choose to serve those in awareness for they shall have a special role in the coming Planet X tribulation a responsibility they assumed before they were ever born. It is why they lead lives of great diversity. Unlike those who seek the safe and predictable comfort of dull repetition.

If you are in awareness, you know it, and you've most likely known it since you were a child. It is why you have always marched to the beat of a different drummer.

No matter what others may say their efforts to dissuade you from your path. Always seem to pass around you, like water passing around a boulder in the midst of the stream yet being an unmovable boulder in the midst of the stream can be a lonely place. This is why a fundamental goal of our mission as a church is to let you know that you are not alone that you do have brothers and sisters in awareness and that they care.

With this in mind, let's examine the three leading causes of death during the tribulation.

3

Three Leading Causes of Tribulation Death

If we are to survive the coming Planet X tribulation we must understand what will prove to be the three greatest causes of death during this time.

The number one cause of death during the Planet X tribulation will be denial. If you're not sure as to what denial means in this context ask someone in awareness with a spoiler spouse, who persistently threatens to divorce them because of their interest in Planet X.

The number two cause of death during the Planet X tribulation will be procrastination. Interestingly enough this is also a big problem for many who are already in awareness. They spend hours each day on social media chasing salacious headlines and mash up of videos of things they've already seen before. Rather than wasting time with these frauds, they could use it more profitably by watching videos about useful survival skills, such as how to sharpen a knife, preserve food, make a fire, and so forth.

The number three cause of death during the Planet X tribulation will be location and it's not a hard thing to figure out. Coastal dwellers have at least a 70% chance of dying during the tribulation, because 70% of the earth is covered with water. For this reason, the most important thing you can do to ensure that you and your loved ones survive the tribulation is to relocate away from a danger zone.

Over the years, I've hosted numerous relocation conferences while these conferences are personalized to the unique requirements of the attendees, I always begin each one by explaining the key things we need to look for in a suitable relocation area. In the second installment in this series, I'll share those relocation insights with you.

But for now, let's return to the number one reason why I founded the knowledge Mountain Church of Perpetual Genesis back in 2015. The fact that in a decade-long tribulation, conventional, me-and-mine survival strategies are nothing more than a long walk off a short pier. To prove the point, let's hunker in the bunker.

4

Survival Groups for a Decade-Long Tribulation

What troubles me most about what I call me-and-mine prepping is that time and again, I see people who are only interested in saving themselves and their loved ones along with a few friends perhaps. It is why I see so many of them building small, me-and-mine survival shelters.

Perhaps that's a good strategy for a few weeks or maybe even a month, but we're talking about a decade-long tribulation, during which you may have to live in your cramped shelter for several months at a time. So in terms of living conditions think about what you're getting into.

A me-and-mine survival shelter is about as comfortable as a World War II diesel submarine. These old submarines would go to sea for approximately 60 to 75 days at a time. After which they would return to port while the submarine was being prepared for the next patrol, the crew could take shore leave and get some relief from the pressures of frequent dangers and confined hardships. With this in mind, how often can a family enjoy shore leave from their me-and-mine shelter stresses?

This is one of the reasons why me-and-mine strategies make no sense to me. I grew up in the West with the lore of pioneers, and the one thing folks understood in those days was practicality. And so, they did not open the West with me-and-mine strategies. Rather, pioneering families banded together in large companies or wagon trains and trekked westward together with a simple understanding. There is strength in numbers. So, when they faced danger, they circled the wagons and covered each other's back.

What I am saying is that what worked for the pioneers will work for us during the tribulation as well. How do we know that? Because these pioneer strategies are tried and true.

But what about me-and-mine survival shelter preppers are these strategies based upon a proven concept. Now these plans are based on Cold War era shelter strategies which rely on a threat matrix from the last century, known as NBC for nuclear, biological, and chemical.

The only difference between then and now, is that NBC is now NBC+E. Nuclear, biological, chemical, plus earthquakes. The assumption is that if you prepare for these four threats, you can expect to survive whatever happens. After that, you'll work things out as you go along.

Unlike the strength in numbers strategies of the pioneers modern, preppers are betting on NBC+E strategies that have never been proven. Why, because they are putting their faith in an assumption. That strength in technology equals strength in numbers.

In terms of a few weeks or months, this assumption can work. But when you're talking about several years, it will certainly fail especially for us folks in the industrialized first world.

Living in push-button information societies, we'll lose so much of what we've become accustomed to having. Consequently, surviving for the sake of survival alone will lead us down a lonely path of lost hope. When that happens, many will lay their heads to sleep with a prayer that "God, I am so weary of this life. Please take me in my sleep."

But for now let's ask the more fundamental question. How will this affect the people who live in the third world countries where life is already hard for them?

The coming tribulation will be another day with a different version of bad. How will they deal with it? As they always do, together as villages and communities.

But in terms of the future, who will be the most capable of re-building the world once we reach what I call the backside? A time when we see blue skies and taste sweet waters once again. Here the answer is clear. This responsibility will fall upon the shoulders of push-button information age survivors. Why, because the having of things is less important than the knowing of things which is what we'll need to rebuild a more modern and sensible world.

Still the same, what about those who ask God to take them in their sleep. If they keep awakening to another day of hopeless misery, how long will it take before they finally do the deed themselves or surrender their lives to those eager to take them.

Conversely, what would give us enough hope that we would not ask God to take us in our sleep? That strength my friends will come from a personal commitment to purposeful survival for an enlightened future. Assuming there is a strategy for this commitment, how will it work?

There is a strategy and I call enlightened continuity and comfort. What is enlightened continuity? It is having a reason to wake up each morning that embraces our noble virtues with a plan for bringing about an enlightened future.

What is enlightened comfort is not about is luxury survival shelters with big screen televisions and hot tubs. That's short-sighted consumer logic.

Rather, there is an ancient wisdom that when things are at their worst, we are at our best. Granted, there'll also be those who follow a dark path of malevolence.

Therefore, enlightened comfort begins with knowing that you are a valued member of a community. One that rewards you with warm smiles when you do the right things and the comfort of warm embraces when you find the strength to endure a hardship. This is the comfort that will matter most.

So then here we have two opposing strategies. On one hand, me-and-mine sheltering or MMS for short. On the other, enlightened continuity and comfort or ECC for short.

What we already know is that MMS is based on unproven Cold War shelter strategies. Conversely, what is ECC based on? Simply put, it is based on the three founding precepts of our church which are self-sufficiency, hope for the future and knowing you are not alone. With this in mind, let's use these three precepts to illustrate the differences between me-and-mine sheltering or MMS and enlightened continuity and comfort, ECC.

Both MMS and ECC view self-sufficiency as absolutely essential, but with ECC the reason goes further. We believe that the independence of self-sufficiency is the foundation of spiritual freedom, which gives our species the ability to advance towards an enlightened future.

Where the two differ first, is with hope for the future. With MMS, it is survival of the fittest. The last ones left standing win. But what is the light at the end of this tunnel? A despotic mad Max world where the downtrodden will lament the end of this civilization? Where is the hope in that?

It is for this reason that we ask each new member of our church to write what we call a Mission Victory plan. A mission victory plan consists of three short statements based on our three precepts and it begins with each member's own journey of awareness.

Then, we ask the member to create a visual image of success in his or her mind about what life will look like on the backside such as happy children at play. And finally, what that member is prepared to do to make his or her vision of success possible.

Remember, during the darkest times of the tribulation, people will lay their heads down with a prayer to God that they perish in their sleep. If they've led a good life, perhaps God will answer that prayer, but if there is something more for them to learn then they'll awaken in the morning. This is when a mission victory plan can help to restore their hope with the promise of a clean slate for the creation of the next civilization and an enlightened future.

The third of the three precepts is knowing you are not alone. We humans are social animals and we instinctively understand the concept of strength in numbers. Yet, me-and-mine survival is akin to living in a big city, where folks go about their daily business with as much separation between themselves and everyone around them as possible.

The same holds true with surviving in small numbers by avoiding detection.

It is naïve thinking because those who want to find you will. Therefore, what avoiding detection really means is that you survive only to live each day with the fear of detection. And what is the light at the end of this tunnel? No doubt, a nagging sense of dread and paranoia.

Again, this brings us back to the Achilles heel of me-and-mine survival strategies. That strength in technology equals strength in numbers. A form of thinking that only results in the false confidence that you can be the master of your own fate during the tribulation.

The fact is there will be no guarantees for anyone during the tribulation, regardless of how much or how little you are prepared. Rather, survival is a heuristic process of learning what hurts and what works with the goal being that, you learn enough about what works before what hurts kills you. And for those who insist on knowing the exact dates or days when something specific is going to happen, this too is part of the same Achilles heel because the universe is not unfolding at the speed of human expectations.

It is for these reasons that each of us needs to know that we are not alone, even when we are surrounded by people. Just ask any teenager in high school who's not desirable enough to run with the right crowd they're ostracized and pushed to the fringes as unappealing geeks or dweebs. Consequently, these poor children walk amongst hundreds of others each day in terrible isolation.

During the tribulation, we can ill afford such childish behavior. Rather, each of us must know and feel with confidence in our hearts that we are valuable members of the community and treasured as such because of the things we do. Likewise, our communities must know they are not alone that there are like-minded communities elsewhere with whom they can share knowledge, resources and to collaborate with for mutual defense.

If you're wondering, where these like-minded survival communities are most likely you'll find one of them just a few minutes away from your home. You see, there will come a time when some leaders in faith-based organizations who trust their instincts will know that they are seeing something in the sky that is a clear and present danger. Likewise, they'll know the time has come to lead their flocks to safety.

Yes, that's right. When we have our last window of opportunity to do something, it will not be our government that helps us. Rather, you will be those who lead us in prayer and who pray alongside us. It is from this seed stock that a national network of faith-based survival communities can and will grow.

5

Three Important Advantages of Faith-Based Survival Communities

Here is the truth of it. Your chances and those of your loved ones to survive the tribulation will be significantly greater as members of a faith-based survival community with 100 or more members, because faith-based organizations have three important advantages.

First is an established chain of command. The number one reason why secular survival communities fail is not their ability to build shelters or to stockpile supplies. This they usually do it very well. Rather, in the absence of a clear and present danger, leadership challenges arise and thereby divide the communities, causing them to fail.

The second is rapid disaster logistics. It can take a church 30 years to build a library, but when disaster strikes, that church will be ready to serve the community in three days or less. Why, because profit is not the incentive.

And finally, a diversity of survival skills remembers this one simple fact of evolution. If you are not resourceful, you die. This means that adapting to tribulation hardships will be less about the having of things and more about the knowing of things. The people you pray with will come from all walks of life, with a myriad of skills, professions, hobbies and affiliations, which is a veritable bounty of human treasure.

So where do you get started? Independent houses of worship will likely be more adaptable to changing circumstances. Visit these churches, attend their services and see if you are comfortable surviving a decade-long tribulation with the members of this congregation. In other words, are they your kind of survival people?

If you do not get a warm and fuzzy feeling about this, move on to the next one. But if you do get a warm and fuzzy feeling, the next step is to take a serious look at the leadership. This is because the leadership of that community will have the greatest impact upon the survivability of all concerned.

6

Identifying Survival-Minded Tribulation Faith Leaders

The last window of opportunity for any group or organization to organize will be when people are looking up at the sky and then turning to mainstream media for an understanding of what they're seeing. When the media tells them that all they're seeing is an interesting light show, then you'll note that this is the last chance to begin preparing. This is when survival minded faith leaders must know in their hearts that they're seeing a clear and present danger and that the time has come to lead their flocks to safety.

To begin, arrange a private meeting with the faith leader during a quiet time of the week and then use a fixed sequence of three probative questions to identify his or her potential as a survival minded faith leader.

I cannot understate the importance of probative questioning, because it is reliable way to measure leaders chances of becoming a successful tribulation leader. If they cannot be attentive, forthright and direct when answering your questions beware they will be weak tribulation leaders.

And yes, asking probative questions may seem awkward but not for those who have been in awareness for many years and who have been expelled from numerous churches in study groups, because they like to ask questions that are questions that are not found on the thou shalt only ask questions from this list, list. So because their questions are off list, they tend to be ostracized for their curiosity. Yet they never give in.

Another danger sign is a spiritual leader who is incredibly adept at dealing with difficult situations by politely sidestepping them or by offering answers that sound intelligent, yet failed to satisfy. I call these lettuce answers because you have to chew an awful lot of lettuce to get a few net calories; so in the end it's just not worth the effort to chew it all.

Therefore, the primary goal of probative questioning is to test for sincerity and honesty with questions designed to provoke body language responses. In other words, body language is more important than verbiage, so what you're looking for are cues. This is a process much akin to that of seasoned poker players. They closely observe other players at the gaming table for what they call "tells" such as how they handle their cards and chips at the table.

With this in mind, here are a few helpful tells to look for when asking a probative questions.

1. Do they avoid eye contact with you by looking away? This is called aversion and it means they're not being completely honest with you.

2. Do they cover their faces? When people are hiding information or their true intentions, they often use their hands to mask their faces.

3. Attentiveness to you and your questions are critical. If they are distracted by fiddling with papers and the such, this behavior suggests a lack of interest or dishonesty.

4. Squared shoulders. When people are withholding information or bluffing, they will avoid facing you with their shoulders square to yours. Rather, they'll angle their shoulders relative to yours. Women are more subtle about this, whereas men are more pronounced.

5. Paralinguistics is how a thing is said. Be mindful of pitch, volume, and intonation of speech. Children intuitively understand that how we say a thing, is more trustworthy than what we say. It is only when we acquire guile as adults that we forget this simple truth of our child. Ergo, listen like a child and trust your instincts.

How effective is this method? To illustrate the point, we'll use airport security as an example. The prevailing logic here in the USA, is that it is better to strip search a grandmother than to profile people. So how is that working for us, let's compare airport security in America with that of Israel.

In a 2015 CNN article titled, *Why Are We Spending $7 Billion on TSA?*, they say as follows: "News that the Transportation Security Administration missed a whopping 95% of guns and bombs in recent airport security red team tests was justifiably shocking. It's clear that we're not getting value for the $7 billion we're paying the TSA annually."

Now let's take a look at the prevailing security logic in Israeli airports.

There, passengers are closely profiled and often subjected to multiple interrogations while standing in line. Israeli security personnel are trained to look for suspicious body language and they use probative questions to profile passengers. Security experts worldwide agree that these controversial Israeli techniques are far more successful than the kinds of predictable checks and scans used by the TSA and at a fraction of the cost.

So with this in mind, let's look at three, simple probative questions to determine if a faith leader is ready to be a survival faith leader.

The first question is "Do you think the weather is getting really strange these days?"

If the answer is something like global warming is nonsense and is accompanied by dismissive and patronizing body language, this is a huge a red flag. Go no further and visit a different congregation.

However, if the faith leader is open to the question look for negative body language signs. Be wary if the faith leader evidences politeness as opposed to a factual interest. If the interest appears sincere, proceed to the second question.

With the second question, you're looking to see if the faith leader is willing to march to the beat of a different drummer. Now you ask about geoengineering, or what is known as chemtrail spraying. If you live in an area where there is routine spraying and the faith leader says I've never noticed it, this is a negative sign. It means the faith leader is so preoccupied with life, that he or she is not looking up to see what's happening above them.

Or, if they respond by saying it is only a foolish conspiracy theory or condensation from international flights and nothing more, than they are ignorant by intention. In this case, go no further and visit a different congregation.

However, if the faith leader expresses any level of concern over geoengineering, or chemtrail spraying, then proceed to the third and final question.

Here planning and preparation is essential as this is an organized form of self-defense question. With this probative question, you're looking to elicit a response to the leaders comfort with the right of self-defense and there are two variants depending on your local jurisdiction.

Before the meeting, check to see if your jurisdiction allows citizens to carry a concealed weapon on their body. For example in Alaska you can carry without a permit, whereas in Nevada, a sheriff must issue what is called a concealed carry weapon permit.

If concealed carry is allowed in some manner in your jurisdiction the first variant of this question is, "How do you feel about members of your congregation, carrying a loaded and concealed weapon to your services?"

However, if you live in a jurisdiction that does not allow its citizens to carry a concealed weapon, use the second variant of this question, "How do you feel about off duty peace officers, carrying a loaded and concealed weapon to your services?"

In either case, be sure to use the word "loaded" as the emotional emphasis of this word, will help to yield a more revealing answer.

In general, what you are looking for is any sign of discomfort or distress as a result of the question. The fact is, many faith leaders across the country will respond positively as most states allow for concealed carry in churches.

There is also more tolerance on the issue now because of the 2015 church shooting in Charleston South Carolina at the Hampstead Church, an African Methodist Episcopal Church. In a heinous attack by a white supremacist, six women and three men were brutally murdered.

Therefore, if you see discomfort or distress, then you know you're looking at a faith leader who will hamper, second guess or overly moralize members of the church with military or paramilitary experience who are acting to keep the community safe. In other words, they will be weak survival faith leaders, and this weakness will only serve to provoke divisive leadership confrontations in the future.

However, if the faith leader answers this question matter-of-factly with respect for the right for people to feel safe from violent perpetrators, then you have found a viable, survival oriented, faith-based organization survival leader to align yourself with.

So what comes next? When the time is right, you do not enter that community from the bottom. Rather, you enter it from the top.

7

Establishing Value with Tribulation Leaders

Have you been in awareness for years, or perhaps since you were a child. If so, you are likely to be a sensitive person who seeks to understand others in a compassionate and holistic way. It is also likely that you, like most Americans struggle to get by each day. It is why those in awareness often voice the same frustration. What's the good of being aware if you cannot afford bullets beans and bunkers? This is the one question the elites want us to ask, whereas God does not.

Later in this series, you'll learn why, and you'll also learn the true purpose of your awareness, a purpose that will make you very valuable to those who can afford mountains of bullets, beans and bunkers. For now, I can share with you a simple plan for survival. One that you will find on the back cover of my book, *Surviving the Planet X Tribulation: A Faith-Based Leadership Guide*. It reads as follows:

"Know this, you are in awareness because God intends for you to be a part of the solution. Read and study this book thoroughly to prepare yourself for your true mission and calling. Then, when a spiritual leader you admire and respect is seeing the same clear and present danger that you are, your path is simple. Hand that leader this book as you say, 'You need a plan, and this is the plan that will work for what is coming. Please read it, and if you have any questions, I am always at your service.'"

So for those of you who are in awareness with big hearts and small wallets what does this mean?

Are you worried for yourself and your loved ones because you cannot afford a mountain of beans? Then prove you are worth your weight in beans by using this book as a bridging tool. It will help you to establish your value as a teacher, mentor and comforter to those whom you are in service to.

By reading and studying this book you'll understand firsthand the true power of the mentoring process. Then, when the time comes, be yourself as you mentor and comfort tribulation leaders through the difficulties of awareness compression. In this way you will gain their confidence, both through your centeredness and through your devotion to serving others.

There it is folks. Follow this plan and you will enter the community from the top, and not the bottom. When you do, the first question will be, "will we live?"

This is a critical question because the tribulation will be a lengthy period of time punctuated by brief cataclysms, claiming thousands if not millions of lives at a time.

But there will come the worst of it all, the Nibiru Pole shift, which will claim billions of lives, and in the second installment of this series we'll talk at length about who will live and who will die during this event.

So until the next time we meet, remember Marshall's motto. Destiny comes to those who listen, and fate finds the rest. So learn what you can learn, do what you can do, and never give up hope! For the knowledge Mountain Church of Perpetual Genesis, I'm Marshall Masters

> ANNOUNCER: This program was made possible by the Knowledge Mountain Church of Perpetual Genesis. To learn more visit knowledgemountain.org. We also encourage you to pursue your awareness path by reading Marshall's book, *Surviving the Planet X Tribulation: A Faith-Based Leadership Guide.* To learn more, visit planetxtribulation.com. Next up in this series is part two, Nibiru Pole Shift – Who Lives, Who Dies.

Nibiru Pole Shift – Who Lives, Who Dies

8

Introduction to Part 2

ANNOUNCER: Welcome to Two Suns in the Sky: Who Lives, Who Dies. To learn more about this three part audiobook series, visit twosunsinthesky.com. And now, part two, Nibiru Pole Shift – Who Lives, Who Dies with author and narrator, Marshall Masters.

Hello, I'm Marshall Masters, chief steward of the knowledge Mountain Church of perpetual Genesis.

In part one of this three part series, purposeful survival for an enlightened future, you learned that as a person in awareness, if you cannot afford to buy a mountain of beans, that's okay. Rather, you need to become worth your weight in beans to the leadership of a faith-based survival community.

In the third and final part of this series, the survival power of perpetual Genesis, you'll learn what that plan entails and how to prepare for your role as a teacher, mentor and comforter.

However in this second part of this series, we're going to answer the one question that will be on everyone's minds once we all see a clear and present danger. That being, will we survive? This is why this second part is titled Nibiru Pole Shift – Who Lives, Who Dies.

With this in mind, let's quickly review the three leading causes of death during the coming tribulation.

The number one cause of death during the Planet X tribulation will be denial. The number two cause of death will be procrastination and the number three cause of death will be location. Especially during the Nibiru pole shift event, so let's take a quick look at that.

9

The Georgia Guidestones and the Nibiru Pole Shift

In 1980 a granite monument was erected in Elbert County, Georgia. We know it today as the Georgia Guidestones and it is inscribed with 10 guidelines in eight different languages: English, Spanish, Swahili, Sanskrit, Hebrew, Arabic, Chinese, and Russian.

What the first guideline tells us is to maintain humanity under half a billion in perpetual balance with nature. What the first guideline does not tell us is how humanity will be reduced to this level. This is important because it will not happen all at once.

Rather, what we'll see during the coming Planet X tribulation is a decade or more of death and suffering where there will be long periods of relative calm, punctuated by brief moments of cataclysm, claiming thousands if not millions of lives at a time.

However, the worst event will be the Nibiru pole shift, or the "days of darkness" as some call it. This is when, Nibiru, the outermost major planet of the Planet X system passes between Earth and the sun. When this happens, billions will die as has been foretold in prophecies, predictions and wisdom texts.

This is why I believe the real message of the Georgia Guidestones is not that nine out of 10 will perish. It is that the one in 10 who do survive the tribulation will do so because they think like survivors. They observe the world about them as it is, formulate a plan and then take action on that plan even though it may not be the best possible choice. Why does this work? Louis Pasteur said it best.

A 19th century French biologist microbiologist and chemist, Pasteur is famous for discovering the principles of vaccination and pasteurization. The key to his success was his powers of observation and so the wisdom he passed down to us, is this. That chance favors the prepared mind.

Evolution tells us that if we want to survive the coming tribulation we must be resourceful or we will die. Yet, 90% or more of all Americans refuse to even take this smallest peak at the evidence of what is coming. Is this by choice, or is this how their brains work? This is the question we'll explore with denial causalities.

10

The Propensity For Widespread Denial and Brain Dominance

Most, who have been in awareness for some time, often were in awareness when they were children. Is this you, and is this awareness more of a curse than a blessing for you? Especially whenever you try and share your awareness with friends and families and to what end? Inevitably, you are mocked, ridiculed and threatened into silence.

If you've never been in a situation like this, what does it feel like if you were in awareness?

It would feel like you are the only one eyed person in a land of the blind and what are the blind telling you? "Hey stupid, get a sharp stick and poke out your one good eye, so you can be clever like the rest of us." That's what it feels like and I am not saying this to be humorous. Rather, I'm stating a scientific fact.

On February 22, 2017, a new study by the American Psychological Association was widely reported by the media. The study drew data from two nationally representative studies involving 2000 adults in Germany and Spain. The results were stunning.

The study found that as many as 90% of test subjects do not want to know about negative events in the future. Interestingly enough, the study also found that as many as 70% felt the same about future positive events. So what about those in awareness?

According to the study, those in awareness are pretty rare especially when you consider that only 10% of the survey participants consistently expressed a desire to know about the future.

Dr. Gerd Gigerenzer, of the Max Planck Institute for Human Development, sums it up perfectly. "Not wanting to know appears counter-intuitive and may raise eyebrows, but deliberate ignorance, as we've shown here, doesn't just exist; it is a widespread state of mind."

What will deniers say about this? The usual, "It's all nonsense, nothing is going to happen and I don't want to hear about it."

But for me, the findings of this study triggered a magnificent epiphany. That only a few of us are hardwired by nature to consider something as violent as the Planet X tribulation. The mechanism is called brain dominance. Once you understand this, you'll understand how precious the gift of awareness is.

Back in 2000, I first became interested in brain dominance, the difference between left brain thinkers and right brain thinkers. Using tests available at the time, I determined that I was actually a whole brain synchronized thinker; that being the left and right hemispheres of my brain were balanced.

With this in mind, let's explore right brain dominance together.

Left brain thinkers tend to be time oriented, logical thinkers. Sequential and analytical by nature, they favor tightly ordered checklists and tend to look at the smaller details before looking at the big picture.

The left hemisphere of our brain controls the right side of our body and other left brain functions include analytical, logic, math and science, number skills, objectivity, reasoning, spoken language and written language.

Right brain thinkers are often more creative than their left brained counterparts and are more likely to call upon their intuition in a given situation than to examine all of the facts. In other words, right brain thinkers tend to trust their gut instinct more than left brain thinkers.

The right hemisphere of our brain controls the left side of our body and other right brain functions include 3D shapes, creativity, emotion, holistic thought, imagination, insight, intuition, music and art awareness and synthesizing.

Whether you are a left brained thinker or a right brain thinker, it is important to note that we need both hemispheres, and proof of this is whole brain synchronization thinkers.

With whole brain synchronization, both hemispheres of the brain are in balance and work in harmony. Interestingly enough, humanity's greatest philosophers, thinkers, inventors, and artists tend to be whole brain synchronized thinkers.

But what about those in awareness did God hardwire them to survive the coming Planet X tribulation. Let's take a hard look at that.

11

Left-brain vs. Right-brain Survival Thinking

Most in awareness are not financially successful people. They have big hearts and small wallets. Therefore, it's no wonder they ask, "If I cannot afford bullets beans and bunkers, is God punishing me?"

If this is you, here's my answer. God is not punishing you. Rather, you just a stranger in a strange land of left-brained people. To help you frame this answer, let's look at some basic differences between left brained and right brained Americans.

Keep in mind, we're speaking in general terms and that there are always exceptions to the rule.

Left brain thinkers do not often rely on intuition or instinct. Rather, they look at facts and tradition.

Right brain dominant people are artistic, innovative and use free association thought processes to achieve originality and inventiveness.

Left brain thinkers generally prefer organized religions because they are predictable and spell out how people should conduct themselves.

Right brain thinkers generally prefer spirituality to the rigid dogma and doctrine of organized religions.

Left brain thinkers tend to use our world to achieve their ends, often at the expense of their own happiness and the environment. Lawyers, judges and bankers tend to be left brain.

Right brain thinkers gravitate to occupations that require creative thinking, perceptiveness and spontaneity, such as politics, acting and athletics.

Right brain thinkers respond to negative feedback and are more likely to cut their losses short, whereas left brain thinkers tend to become locked into a narrow point of view where they limit themselves to doing things the way they've been done before.

Left brain thinkers become expert at denying anything is wrong or of having made a wrong decision. Ergo, left brain thinkers can be ever optimistic, even while stepping off a cliff. In other words, a left brain thinker jumping off a 20 story office building can be totally convinced that he or she is flying for the first 19 floors on the way down.

As someone in awareness, are you an exception and are there others like you hear I can shed some interesting light on the question. As I mentioned earlier, in 2000, I first became interested in brain dominance.

Since then, I've informally profiled interactions with those in awareness who contacted me through my research and publishing efforts on my website Your Own World USA [Yowusa.com] to assess their brain dominance. Again, it was never a formal study. Rather, I was just curious in the information for myself.

Now for the very first time, I want to share the general results. This is because those who are spiritually drawn to the Knowledge Mountain Church of Perpetual Genesis present the very same brain dominance patterns that I saw with those drawn to my science publishing efforts for the last 15 years. In other words, whether folks are drawn to my work for reasons of science or spirituality makes no difference.

The two other significant trends I've observed over the years are: The distribution patterns never vary and the more people I've profiled, the easier it became.

12

Right-brain Awareness and Planet X Precognition

Let's examine the brain dominance results of my informal study of those in awareness about the coming Planet X flyby, beginning with the left brain thinkers.

One constant throughout the years has been that only 5% of the people who are aware of Planet X are left brain thinkers. I call them the perceptiveness, because they usually do not come to the topic through dreams visions and premonitions as others do. Rather, they observe the world as it is and how it relates to their risk posture. Most often, this is because of their profession, where they take risks, evaluate risks or manage risks. Now, let's look at whole brain synchronized thinkers.

As a group, whole brain synchronized thinkers tend to come from highly technical fields and those dealing with the arts. This group constitutes 20% of all the people with an interest in Planet X.

And finally, let's move on to right brained thinkers. Right brain thinkers constitute the vast majority of people with an awareness of the coming tribulation. They represent 75% of the people I come into contact with on this topic. Unlike the left brained people in awareness, or perceptiveness as I call them, the right brain super majority often struggles to survive.

So now you know the brain dominance statistical breakdown for everyone who is following my work on the coming Planet X tribulation. With this in mind, I want to focus on the most intriguing statistical dichotomy presented in this program.

Only 5% of the people who follow my work on Planet X are left brain thinkers. Keep that number in mind as we compare this small minority of those who follow my work with the total population of the United States.

When we do, the numbers literally flip-flop because 95% of all Americans are left brain thinkers. This is important because this statistic brings us back to the study published by the American Psychological Association on February 22, 2017.

According to that study, as many as 90% of the test subjects did not want to know about negative events in the future. Given that 95% of all Americans are left brain thinkers, the numbers correlate when it comes to Planet X. Those most likely to be in denial will be left brain dominant.

Yet oddly enough, intelligence agencies in America, Russia and elsewhere appreciate the value of right brain thinkers. It is why they use psychics and remote viewers. Both paranormal intelligence gathering techniques are highly effective and the only real difference is preference. American intelligence agencies prefer remote viewers over psychics and the reverse is true for the Russian intelligence agencies.

While the techniques differ, both use the right hemisphere of the brain. This is because the right hemisphere of the brain is what I call a cosmic transceiver.

For those of you in awareness, you need to understand that psychics and remote viewers employed by these agencies only use a limited amount of their God-given right brain functionality and when they do, just for specific purposes.

Why do American intelligence agencies prefer remote viewers over psychics? While psychics must be right brain dominant, remote viewers can be left brain dominant, because they only use a limited and specific portion of their right brain functionality. I call these the lower right brain functions.

So, why is it that left brain dominant thinkers appear to be hardwired for denial?

Again we go back to the observation of Dr. Gerd Gigerenzer of the Max Planck Institute who makes the case for left brained thinker denial when he says, "deliberate ignorance, as we've shown here, doesn't just exist; it is a widespread state of mind."

Furthermore, his observation of "deliberate ignorance" clearly applies to America's left brained majority, which in turns raises an existential, life or death question. Who will live and who will die?

Before we tackle that question, we need to examine the number two cause of death during the coming Planet X tribulation, that being procrastination.

13

Procrastination and First Lady Eleanor Roosevelt

No matter how vociferous one is in protecting their bliss of ignorance with denial, it can all end in a very unsettling instant. One day you see something that strikes you as being out of place and ask that point-of-no-return question. What exactly am I looking at? This is when your denial ends and awareness begins and frankly it's never a pleasant experience.

Awareness comes to us in many different ways but the experience is always the same. You're "salmon slapped" as I call it, because you feel like you've just been slapped upside the head with a dead salmon and there you are, spitting scales and wondering just what happened.

But awareness does not mean that you're ready to take action. In fact many people who come into awareness use procrastination to cope with their new reality. They assure themselves that if they just observe the situation without taking action, that they are doing something constructive. It is like nailing one foot to the floor. No matter how much you spin around, the scenery never changes.

This is why procrastination will be the number two cause of death during the coming Planet X tribulation.

Yes, people will know the truth, but they will fail to take constructive action because they do not want to admit to themselves that life as we know it is coming to an end. This is hope against hope, a desperate belief that by some remote fraction of a possibility, nothing will happen. Yet it will.

For me, I've thought about procrastination since I was a boy of nine. That was when I first learned that all of my relatives on my mother's side in Europe died in the Nazi concentration camps. It is a sobering thing to learn that an entire branch of your family tree is as lifeless as the cold vacuum of deep space.

I'll never know their names or anything about them, but one thing I know is this. I do love them very much and my will to honor their sacrifice has given me the tenacity to continue my research since 2000.

Yet, I often wonder. Could there have been an alternate outcome for my relatives in 1933, the year German President Hindenburg named Adolf Hitler as the Führer?

I often wondered had they read Mein Kompf? Published in 1925, in it Hitler said "I believe that I am acting in accordance with the will of the Almighty Creator: by defending myself against the Jew, I am fighting for the work of the Lord."

How many of my relatives in 1933 had hoped against hope that the German people would not be lured in by Hitler's anti-Semitic rants, that the German people were too dignified and noble for such a thing. That it was better to procrastinate by observing future developments. But how long could this strategy go on?

Most likely, that period of procrastination ended in 1938 during the Kristallnacht, the night of the broken glass, when the

Nazis unleashed a national campaign of violence against Jews in Germany. "Fighting for the work of the Lord," as Hitler put it. The Nazis burned synagogues everywhere and shops were wrecked. The contents looted as thousands of Jews were arrested. Yes. By that time, it was too late for deniers and procrastinators alike.

And so the question nags me. What if my relatives had been ready to imagine the unimaginable in 1933 and had the courage to take action? How many of them could have survived the Holocaust?

So here we are, and there is an old saying, "what goes around comes around." Perhaps we need to ask ourselves, who amongst us is willing to imagine the unimaginable and to take action? This is the real question of our time and it is not a question intended for a minority, but rather, each and every one of us. What should we do?

A former American First Lady gave us the answer, long before Adolf Hitler's rise to power. Eleanor Roosevelt said, "You must do the thing you think you cannot do." It was wise advice indeed.

Keep her advice in mind as we now answer the existential question. Who lives and who dies.

14

Who Lives, Who Dies – Can You Handle the Truth?

So who lives and who dies? Let's begin with the ones most likely to die.

Earlier we learned that we live in a country where 95% of the people are left brain thinkers and where 90% of the people tell those of us in awareness, that the coming Planet X tribulation is all nonsense. That nothing is going to happen and that they do not want to hear about it.

Where does this toxic combination of denial logic and left brained thinking come from? Perhaps it's not something we're born to do, but rather, taught to do.

America's public schools systems are heavily influenced by the Prussian education system reforms of the late 18th and early 19th centuries, the goal being to teach children and young adults to be obedient to authority. Consequently, those who graduate these schools do so, with a heavy orientation towards left brain thinking, the kind that rewards Western consumer societies with left brain thinking workers and consumers.

On the other hand, homeschooled children are better educated and less likely to become mechanistic and procedure bound.

Is there a terrible truth here? That the vast majority of Americans are destined to fail? Something I call "failure programming."

Is this why the three major causes of tribulation death denial, procrastination, and location will eventually claim billions of lives during the coming Planet X tribulation.

If so, is there an intentional plan at work, one no less malevolent than Adolf Hitler's final solution. Assuming so, this time it is different that the target is not a minority, but rather, our species as a whole.

Let's assume that this is so. Who would do it? The one percent of the one percent who controls our world from the shadows, and their aims are not to save the world from human overpopulation, though they will be sure to posit that explanation.

No, their aim is to reduce global population so they can restore their enslavement of our species after the tribulation has passed.

You may be shaking your head in disbelief, and if so, I too once felt this way. That it was inconceivable for me that a premeditated inhumanity on such a vast global scale could be possible. But in time I came to understand that it is 1933 all over again and each of us must choose.

For this reason, I am not going to ask you to imagine the unimaginable. This is a substantial reality you need to find on your own. But there is something I can share with you as a researcher and analyst. A technique I learned a long time ago. It is how you find a great truth, because the greatest truths are by and of necessity – simple.

You begin with a spot, a single point of truth. To visualize this process, let's imagine a large picture puzzle. When we dump all the pieces onto a tabletop what is the first thing we do? We search out the four corners of the puzzle, because we know each of these pieces will lead us to all the others so that we can complete our picture puzzle.

In other words a single point of truth is merely the corner piece of the picture puzzle. Find that corner piece, and everything else will eventually connect to it. To illustrate the concept, let's make a left brained quilt.

We live in a left-brained society with numerous hobbies and pursuits that help us to focus on things other than the dark days coming, like quilting. A time honored tradition that produces wonderful things. As such, we could say that while we use our right brains to design the quilt, the truth, is that we spend most of our time using our left brains to stitch it together.

But how does a right brain thinker see that same quilt?

A right brain thinker also sees a pattern, but one deceptively engineered by the elites who control this world and who want to ensure the deaths of his many people as possible during the coming Planet X tribulation. And so the end product of all of our wonderfully distracted left brain quilting is that we wind up in a left-brained slaughterhouse.

Now we are ready to answer the question. Who lives and who dies? The answer as I call the greatest truths is simple. That those most likely to live will have the courage to imagine the unimaginable, because we must do the things we think we cannot do, a talent more natural to right-brained thinkers.

For this reason those most likely to survive the coming Planet X tribulation will be synchronized whole brain and right brain thinkers.

However, the point of this program is not fear. It is hope for the future. With this in mind, I'm now going to empower you with a positive message about location.

15

Why Location Causes 70% of Tribulation Deaths

The number three cause of death during the Planet X tribulation will be location. Especially during the Nibiru pole shift event which will claim billions of lives. Why? Because as we learned in part one of this series, the vast majority of humanity lives along the shorelines of a major body of water. These large bodies of water account for 70% of the Earth's surface and interestingly enough, here is where the incidence of denial is at its highest.

Most coastal dwellers not only refuse awareness but tend to suppress the awareness of those close to them with angry rants. "It's all nonsense, nothing is going to happen and I do not want to hear about it."

There are reasons why people cling with such fierce intolerance to their denial such as the cost of relocation. They know that moving to safer areas in land will entail a loss of income, status, and a burdensome distance from their networks of families and friends. Therefore, the failure to relocate is rooted in the first and second causes of tribulation death, denial and procrastination.

With this in mind, I'm now going to share with those of you who are ready to actively seek relocation some of the basics I share with those who attend my relocation conferences.

16

Identifying and Evaluating Potential Relocation Areas

The Internet is a wonderful tool for identifying potential relocation areas. However, nothing can replace the efficacy of boots on the ground inspections. Here are the basic guidelines I frequently share with others.

Location, location, location: Seek remote areas away from major cities. The further, the better and look for areas where county building codes and permitting processes are not excessively restrictive. Local culture is important. Look for neighborly people with a positive affinity for families and the land.

Also, remember that after the power grid collapses, city dwellers will flood the surrounding landscape like locust and they're not going to be interested in having meaningful and enlightened conversations about sharing what you have? With this in mind, remember that until you've established yourself in a new community, you too will be viewed by the locals as a locust.

Distance: Remember, location kills, so distance is vital. Seek areas that are 150 miles from any major body of water such as an ocean or great lake. For smaller bodies such as lakes and rivers, if you are close to the water level elevation, determine the widest part of the water body, and locate your shelter at least twice that distance away from it. Also, keep your distance from areas that flood and are subject to heavy seasonal water flows.

Nuclear Power Generating Plants: On March 11, 2011, the world watched in horror as hydrogen explosions tore through the Fukushima Daiichi plant. Since then, it has become an unstoppable nuclear volcano that is killing the Pacific Ocean. During the tribulation, we can expect to see scores of Fukushimas is in the United States and elsewhere in the world. This is because when you shut a reactor down, the core still needs to be cooled for another few years. When the national grid fails, there will eventually be no power to operate the water pumps to do that. This is when, the worst happens.

For this reason, use the following guidelines for avoiding radiation death and cancers. Locate at least 50 miles upwind of and 100 miles downwind any nuclear power generating plant or nuclear weapons research and development facility.

Fracking Wells and Chemical Plants: The concrete casings on fracking wells are designed to last 30 years in normal use. However, some fail on the first day of operation. When severe earthquakes occur on fault lines like the New Madrid, everyone in the country will feel the ground shake.

This is when earthquake-related failures in fracking wells and chemical plants will cause entire regions to become unlivable. For this reason, when you see burning water and dead land, keep moving on.

It will take nature a few centuries to restore the health of these poisoned lands and there are no simple rules of thumb for locating these threats, but what you can do is to begin by locating all fracking wells and chemical plants in areas of potential relocation.

Then determine the aquifers and water tables below them and seek professional help in determining safe distances. Better yet, avoid these areas altogether.

Elevation: Locate in areas that are between 2000 to 4000 feet above sea level. High altitude farming above 5000 feet is not for amateurs because of a short growing season.

Soft Earth: Expect solar radiation and drought to cause defoliation, soil degradation, and the certification this is why you want to locate in an area with rich soil and deep-rooted trees that are drought resistant. Be sure to look for tree species with deep roots.

The point here is that whether or not the trees survive, what matters, is that the soil does.

Topography: Locate on rolling hills midway up from a valley floor and avoid hilltops. Hilltops are difficult to access and stony which makes them difficult for cultivation and vulnerable to hypervelocity winds.

Likewise, avoid steep hillsides. This is because of mud lahars. Also, avoid plains and flatlands because of widespread grass fires, and hypervelocity winds.

Ample Water: You want streams springs, lakes, and artesian wells. No sloughs or swamps or any area where water is still or moves very slowly. These slow-moving areas will stay polluted and will not recover for several decades. As to water wells, you can get hand pumps that will pull water from as deep as 300 feet. Below that you need to use powered mechanical pumps. So, make sure you have wells with sweet water that can support a hand pump.

Security: When evaluating properties make sure you have a member of the team with field combat experience such as an

NCO or an officer. There will be issues of concern for them and you need to listen to their advice.

For example when preparing a property, cut back the tree line in every direction from your shelter to a distance of 100 yards so that you have a 360° clear field of fire.

Observation Vantage Points: The ideal property either commands the high ground or is at least one mile away from an overlooking mountaintop with an unobstructed line of sight. Remember, you will be surveilled from a high ground position if the hostiles have a clear line of sight. Better yet, your community will have radio equipped observation teams positioned on those overlooking hilltops.

Keep your distance from Walmart stores. They will be forward operating bases for Homeland security. Also, avoid properties adjoining a public crossroads where warlords, militias, and military will usually set up checkpoints to arrest people and to confiscate their property and vehicles.

Road Access: You need a level, serviceable entry road leading into your property, such as a paved or gravel road for all season access. It will be essential for heavy vehicles to have ingress to your community for construction, supply delivery and so forth.

Nonetheless be ready to build tank traps into the road, if it becomes necessary to make it impassable for any vehicle.

Due Diligence: On a land reconnaissance, you will typically work with real estate agents. Always ask for a topographical and aerial maps and disclosures of all other information relevant to the property. Also, see if test results on the property are available such as water, leach field, etc.

With wells, you should take a basic water test kit with you to evaluate its pot ability for yourself. You will also need to determine water flow.

Deal with Experts: A land reconnaissance team should have one or more members with backgrounds in defensive security, fire and rescue, agriculture, permit culture, real estate law, hydrology or well drilling, geology and civil engineering.

And there you have it, Marshall's basic relocation guidelines. As a final thought, remember to trust your instincts. If after doing your analysis a location doesn't feel like it is where you need to be, then no matter how sweet the deal is, it's not the right deal for you.

On the other hand, if you find yourself in a place where every fiber of your being tells you that this is where you need to be, then make the call. After that, no matter what others may think of your relocation decision, stand your ground if all they can offer are personal preferences and opinions.

Remember, survival is about three abilities. First, your ability to quickly and accurately assess your situation. Second, your ability to formulate a plan. And third, your ability to take action on that plan even if it is not the best possible plan. There are no guarantees, just the guts to lead decisively.

In the third and final part of this three part series, the survival power of perpetual Genesis and going to share insights with you to help others as a teacher, mentor and comforter so that they can lead decisively.

So until the next time we meet, remember Marshall's motto. Destiny comes to those who listen, and fate finds the rest. So learn what you can learn, do what you can do, and never give up hope. For the knowledge Mountain Church of perpetual Genesis, I'm Marshall Masters.

ANNOUNCER: This program was made possible by the Knowledge Mountain Church of Perpetual Genesis. To learn more visit knowledgemountain.org. We also encourage you to pursue your awareness path by reading Marshall's book, *Surviving the Planet X Tribulation: A Faith-Based Leadership Guide*. To learn more, visit planetxtribulation.com. Next up in this series is part three, The Survival Power of Perpetual Genesis.

The Survival Power of Perpetual Genesis

17

Introduction to Part 3

ANNOUNCER: Welcome to Two Suns in the Sky: Who Lives, Who Dies. To learn more about this three part audiobook series, visit twosunsinthesky.com. And now, part three, The Survival Power of Perpetual Genesis with author and narrator, Marshall Masters.

Hello, I'm Marshall Masters, chief steward of the knowledge Mountain Church of Perpetual Genesis

In part one of this three-part series, *Purposeful Survival for an Enlightened Future*; you learned that as a person in awareness, it does not matter if you cannot afford to buy a mountain of beans. This is because you were shown a plan on how to become a valued member of a faith-based survival community and how to profile potential tribulation leaders so that you could be worth your weight in beans.

I also pointed out in the first part, that we do not use the term tribulation in any biblical or judgmental sense. Rather, we use it exactly as the word tribulation is defined in the dictionary, that being a severe trial or suffering.

In part two of this series Nibiru Pole Shift – Who Lives, Who Dies, you learned about the three major causes of tribulation death, denial, procrastination and location, and how the vast majority of humanity is destined to fall victim to these causalities. Something I call "failure programming" and it is the principal mechanism of denial and procrastination.

An example of failure programming includes fixed outcome beliefs that completely ignore an important law of survival that if you are not resourceful, you die.

Fixed outcome beliefs are typically rooted in theories that maintain a last minute intervention will occur. Those who subscribe to these will be moved out of harm's way at the last minute by divine beings, ancestors, extraterrestrials, multidimensional beings and so forth.

Therefore a basic tenet of these fixed outcome beliefs is that resourcefulness is irrelevant for those willing to put all their options into a single fixed outcome basket. To that, we say, best of luck.

This is why in the final part of this three-part series, were going to offer an alternative to fixed outcome belief systems I call it, Perpetual Genesis and it is much more than a philosophy. It is a cosmic tribulation toolkit for those in awareness who have committed themselves to the role of being teachers, mentors, and comforters.

You will also learn specific ways to use the survival power of Perpetual Genesis. To help faith-based survival community leaders to free themselves from failure programming so they can become more effective in leading their flocks to safety. I'll also share with you body, mind, and soul insights to make you an effective and beloved boots on the ground member of a survival community.

With this in mind, let's quickly review the survival strategy of enlightened continuity and comfort we learned about in the first part of this series.

18

Enlightened Continuity and Comfort (ECC) – Historical Efficacy and Survival Safety

In the first part of this series we introduced the strategy of enlightened continuity and comfort or ECC for short, which is based on the three founding precepts of our church. Those are self-sufficiency, hope for the future and knowing you are not alone.

Now let's bring this down to a first contact level where you as someone in awareness will be a teacher, mentor and comforter for the leadership of a survival community.

Remember, as someone in awareness you're not coming into the community from the bottom, but rather the top. With this in mind, let us now compare these two strategies, using the following three criteria historical efficacy, survival safety and long-term strategy.

When we look at the criteria of historical efficacy, two keywords jumped out at us. Unproven and proven.

Me-and-mine strategies are based on unproven Cold War sheltering strategies which mean that there is no historical basis that proves these strategies can produce a desired or intended result.

Conversely, look at a map and the conclusion with ECC is self-obvious. What the history shows us here is that American Pioneer survival strategies are proven. This is because they did produce desired and intended results.

The next criteria, survival safety, is literally an apples and oranges comparison with technology on one side and numbers on the other.

For example, me-and-mine preppers rely heavily on technology to overcome the weakness of their small numbers. It is why they purchase expensive assault rifles, with custom barrels, scopes, extended magazines and so forth.

Expensive, state of the art weapons may offer a sense of comfort, but what happens when your 14-year-old goes to sleep on guard duty with a very expensive rifle laying across his or her lap. The best case in that situation is everyone survives the nap; worst case, you all die badly.

On the other hand you belong to a survival community of 100 people who cannot afford rifles costing thousands of dollars. Rather your community has a mix of vintage World War II bolt action rifles costing a few hundred dollars for hunting and self-defense.

Now imagine that you are a hostile and you want what is in that shelter or community. You look one way through your binoculars and you see an exhausted 14-year-old on guard duty, holding a $3000 rifle and he or she is beginning to nod off. What are your chances of success there?

Conversely, you look the other way through your binoculars and see 10 alert and vigilant adults holding old, inexpensive 30 caliber bolt action military rifles loaded with inexpensive surplus ammunition.

Now the time has come to decide who you will attack. Do you attack 10 adults with old 30 caliber military rifles or a sleepy 14-year-old holding a state of the art, $3000 rifle?

The choice is obvious. Hostiles may be dumb, but they're not stupid. They can count and one sleepy shooter is easier to outmaneuver than 10 alert shooters, regardless of the technology.

The third criteria is the long term strategy.

With unproven me-and-mine strategies the goal is to survive the initial event. After that, you work things out as you go along. However, this is when the future becomes less focused and more fuzzy.

The single greatest failing of this simplistic logic is the assumption that we only need to survive one major catastrophic event. That's typical disaster thinking. Not tribulation thinking, because we'll have long periods of relative quiescence that will be punctuated by brief moments of cataclysm. This awareness is the very foundation upon which the strategy of enlightened continuity and comfort rests. So what does this all boil down to?

Me-and-mine strategy thinkers will survive the initial event and while they are busy congratulating themselves for being clever, they'll likely be blindsided by the next major cataclysm of the tribulation.

On the other hand, those who embrace the strategy of enlightened continuity and comfort will likewise survive the initial event. However, instead of congratulating themselves, they will be busy using the next period of quiescence, to prepare themselves for the next major cataclysm event.

Here is where you will play a vital role by being in service to the leadership of a faith-based survival community, especially at the outset.

19

The Allure of a Misleading Conventional Wisdom

When you first encounter leaders at the initial stage, expect them to be focused on immediate issues of concern using what folks refer to as conventional wisdom. This is a pitfall, because there is nothing conventional about wisdom. It is wise or unwise and that is all. However, the lure of conventional wisdom is that it can make unwise options appear attractive.

To illustrate the point, let me share with you one of the deadliest conventional wisdom mistakes I see people make.

We learned in part two of our series that left brain thinkers comprise 95% of the American population and that 90% of all Americans do not want to know about bad news in their future. Consequently, the vast majority of Americans are more likely to be in denial and will therefore be more likely to perish in the coming tribulation.

However, sometimes they do experience a brief moment of awareness and since 95% of all Americans are left brained consumers there is a quick fix to calm these fleeting moments of uncertainty. If they buy something, they'll feel better. That's the fix.

It happens when doubts about the future compel them to drive to the store and buy what conventional wisdom tells them is a survival food. Those five gallon buckets of freeze-dried emergency food that offer consumers a big bang for the buck with light weight, long shelf life, convenient prepackaged meals and lots of calories for very little money.

What's not to like? Actually, quite a bit.

While the companies who sell these freeze-dried foods often have the word "survival" in their company name, they always use the term emergency food instead of survival food, and for good reason. It is not survival food.

If you take a close look at the small print, you'll see that most of the calories in these five gallon buckets comes from vegetables, soups, and drinks as opposed to protein sources. Yet, the conventional wisdom shopper allure of these products persists. Why?

Now let's take a closer look at this with the help of the late great comedian, George Carlin.

"Everybody's got to have to have a little place for their stuff. That's all life is about. That's the meaning of life. Trying to find a place to keep your stuff. That's all your house is. Think of it. That's all your house is. A place to keep your stuff."

Now let's take a look at this from the perspective of an enlightened continuity and comfort strategist. What conventional wisdom consumers continually fail to do is to consider the circumstances under which they'll use their emergency food and how.

After all we do live in a modern world. Turn a handle and there is water. Choose a heat setting and you're cooking on the stove top. It all works now, so why shouldn't it work later. This is conventional wisdom.

What is not conventional is an emergency where all of our switches, levers and handles become useless decorations and given that the majority of humanity lives along a coastline, that means that tribulation emergencies will include sudden evacuations as well.

With this in mind, let's go on the road and take the stuff out of the five gallon bucket and use it under these circumstances. In this case, there is an old saying; water is life so this is the first issue.

As a general rule of thumb, it takes one cup of portable water to rehydrate one ounce of freeze-dried food. In other words, you need approximately one canteen of water for each family member for each meal. This during a time when there is no turning a kitchen tap for water and bottled water has long disappeared from store shelves. Now you're going to have to find it, and purify it, and if you think boiling water is all you need to do to make it safe to drink, you're wrong.

In order to prepare your freeze-dried emergency meal, you're also going to need fuel for a fire which means you're going to have to spend time foraging about for firewood. This on top of all of the time you need to spend finding and purifying potable water so that you can rehydrate your freeze-dried emergency food.

Then you have to prepare your freeze-dried meal over a campfire which means you are cooking. During the day, people can see the smoke from your fire. At night, they will see the light from your campfire. Either way, if they are half starved to death, they'll know that you are preparing a meal and where to find you. Then it's guess who's coming to dinner.

Do you really believe that half-starved people are going to walk into your campsite and say, "Oh my, you're so clever; we just wanted to come by and congratulate you before we all go off and starve to death?"

The point here is that these freeze-dried products are designed for camping during good times. Therefore one should not confuse freeze-dried camping food with freeze-dried emergency food.

This is why it is better to stockpile survival foods you do not have to rehydrate or cook, whether they be MREs, meals ready to eat, or canned food. You will be able to eat them quickly without exposing yourself to harm or wasting the better part of your day fetching fuel, and water, and then cooking meals.

That being said, there are excellent uses for freeze-dried foods during the tribulation. For safe shelter locations, these products offer an excellent way to store protein, such as eggs, meat, fish and fowl. As to the high-calorie, low-protein drinks and soups in these buckets, this will become the junk food of the tribulation.

The point here is that you should stockpile high-protein freeze-dried foods for your survival shelter or bunker, because they offer to long term asset advantages. First, they will offer an excellent source of protein for the lean times and second. When things eventually become better, they will become a very valuable form of barter currency, more valuable than gold and silver.

However, as someone in awareness, the most important long term asset you can possess is the survival power of Perpetual Genesis.

20

Freedom and Ascension – The Philosophy of Perpetual Genesis

Perception is everything, and the philosophy of Perpetual Genesis offers a unique perspective on what is going to happen and your role in it. I discussed this philosophy in my book *Surviving the Planet X Tribulation a Faith-Based Leadership Guide;* so, let me focus briefly on the key points relevant to this program.

Most mainstream religions have a terrestrial view of God. There is ourselves, our houses of worship, our nations, and so forth. Beyond all of that is God. On the other hand Perpetual Genesis offers a cosmic view of ourselves and God, and it begins with three simple questions. Where does God live, what does God do, and what has this got to do with me?

For those of you who are still wrestling with the question, does God really exist, there is an old expression. There are no atheists in a foxhole. For those in our church, God is a given and a very real one at that. If you haven't figured this out by now, all we can do is wish you the best of luck.

This now brings us to the first question. Where does God live? We know that we live within God's Creation but where does God live within all that there is. That being the endless void, which extends far beyond the reality of the Creation, we exist within.

This is because our world and all the stars that twinkle at night above our heads, only represent about 5% of all there is. Ergo, Creation occupies a portion of the endless void of the cosmos which is comprised of dark energy and dark matter. The other 95% of all there is. Therefore, while we live within the Creation of God, God lives within the endless void of the cosmos.

Ergo, God is not all there is. Rather, God is continually expanding Creation into the void, which brings us to the second question. What does God do?

To all things there is a purpose and God's mission is the perpetual creation of life from the lifelessness of the void - hence the term, Perpetual Genesis.

One cannot create something from nothing, which is an important fact when we talk about God's purpose. So how is creation made? It is made from the vast unlimited expanse of dark energy and dark matter that fills the entire void.

This is why freedom is vital to God's mission.

Without freedom, there is no free will and free will is the energizing force of intention. This is vital because it is through an act of intention that a universe with its own physical laws can become part of the ever expanding multiverse we call, Creation.

This brings us to the third question of Perpetual Genesis. What has this got to do with me?

Well, what is has to do with you is that you must make an eternal choice as an eternal being.

When you say to God, "I'm with you," this is when you become a Perpetual.

The pledge is simple. "God, today I'm incarnated in this body, on this planet and in this time. When my job of being in service to your mission is completed here, then put me where you need me no matter which universe, time, planet or species. I will hit the ground running and never look back."

As Perpetuals, how do we serve God's mission in this time, on this world, and incarnated in this species? We do it by helping this species along its path of ascension; so that it may become more enlightened and therefore more effective in serving God's mission of Perpetual Genesis.

At present, humanity stands at the threshold of ascension, and here is the silver lining in this dark cloud of tribulation during this suffering. Our species will be freed from the shackles of slavery so that we may ascend beyond the exploitation and subjugation of empire to a new existence, one where acquisition is no longer our driving motive.

So, how will we know if we have achieved this? That we have truly ascended as a species? That is simple. Our driving motive will become that of harmony. Harmony within ourselves and all that it's about us.

Herein, is a classic conflict of good and evil that is happening with our species at this time. Dark entities exist on the physical as well as many other planes and their battle against our ascension is an existential one for them, because we are their primary source of life force energy.

Life force energy only comes from following the path of light and love to God and dark entities can neither make it nor exist without it. Starved of life force energy, they will inevitably sink into the inky blackness of oblivion, there to meet their final fate death eternal. It is why they need to steal life force energy from us by fomenting the worst within us. When they do, it is easy for them to suckle our energy.

But when we ascend as is our right as a species, we will be beyond their dark manipulations and they will lose a major food source. This is why humanity now faces a momentous conflict of good and evil. If we ascend, we free ourselves of these parasites. But if they can hold us back they know they'll be able to milk us to satisfy their own needs, for countless generations of humanity to come.

Obviously, these dark entities will not sink quietly into the darkness of oblivion. And for those of us in awareness as Perpetuals, we know who we must oppose and what must be done. Yet, with a heavy burden of this momentous responsibility comes a joyful life-affirming hope for freedom and ascension.

This is the cosmic perception of Perpetual Genesis. One that fills us with a greater purpose and the will to overcome the hardships of the tribulation.

For those of you in awareness as teachers, mentors, and comforters, this philosophy of Perpetual Genesis will likely be seen as an overreach. So use discretion in sharing this knowledge. Make sure that those you gift with this knowledge are ready to receive it.

As for the rest, remember that Perpetual Genesis is more than a philosophy. It is a toolkit. And to see some of the other tools, let's organize our toolkit into three simple categories that everyone can understand and agree upon: Mind, body, and soul.

With that, let's begin with the mind.

21

Your Cosmic Transceiver – Its Use Navigating the Tribulation

Let's imagine that you need to sail hundreds of miles across the Pacific Ocean in a small boat with absolutely no navigational aids whatsoever. A left-brained thinker will likely say, "You mean no GPS navigation. Not even a compass and sextant? Are you crazy? You'll get lost and die out there!" And you know; for left brain thinkers that makes perfect sense.

But the ancient Polynesian people did exactly that. In fact they were the first humans to navigate by the rising and setting points of the stars and by observing ocean swells, currents, and prevailing winds. This is how they used their left brain.

But all of that could not have worked without their vital right brain functions. Because they use their ability to memorize every way point of their journey, a right brain process of using images to form precise memories. This in turn enabled them to internalize the clock of the universe. A very right brain holistic application of synthesis through insight and perception.

No doubt, if the ancient Polynesian navigators could be tested today for brain dominance metrics, the question would not be how many of them were left brain dominant. Rather, the question would be how many of them were balanced whole brain or right brained dominance thinkers?

This is because they use their right brain functions to closely observe and analyze the environment and navigated with a holistic understanding of ocean currents, prevailing winds and so forth. This is why these ancient mariners were so successful in populating so many small islands in the largest ocean on our planet. And yet they were only using a portion of their right brain functions. So have things changed? No.

In part two of this series, we learned that American intelligence agencies favor the use of remote viewers. Like the Polynesian navigators they to only use a portion of their right brain functions. But what about accessing and using all of our lower and higher right brain functions?

For those of you in awareness, here is some good news. You are not encumbered by earthly limitations. Rather, you have the ability to use the cosmic transceiver in your right brain for both the lower and higher functions.

What does that mean?

The higher function of your right brain cosmic transceiver enables you to create two-way ethereal connections across the veil to the other side. Regardless of what you call it, God, Yahweh, divine guides, and so forth, your right brain cosmic transceiver offers you unlimited access to the other side for divine help and inspiration. This kind of empowerment is life-changing and if you are just starting out, let me give you a suggestion.

Psychic techniques such as channeling and auto-writing are the most powerful, but they are risky. This is because if you do not know how to shield yourself, you can be manipulated by dark entity impostors. So these powerful techniques are not something you want to learn on your own. Rather, you need to learn these techniques with the help of an advanced mentor.

This is why I suggest that you begin with remote viewing. This technique does not expose you to the impostor risk, and is a powerful way to learn the self-discipline needed for more advanced techniques such as channeling and auto-writing.

There are excellent seminars and home study courses offered on the Internet. I personally learned remote viewing in a seminar offered by Major Ed Dames, and I know without a doubt, this is a very powerful survival skill – that is well worth your time to learn.

However, even before you begin any formal studies, there is something enjoyable you can begin doing today. It is a sample 10-step meditation exercise I've created to help you access your lower and higher right brain functions more effectively.

You may be thinking why meditation? It is because experts agree that meditation is the best way to enhance your right brain functionality. If you are already using a meditation technique or are trained in one that you like, you can adapt it to this 10-step program which is designed to enhance your right brain functionality for tribulation survival needs.

For this presentation I am going to use Danjeon Breathing a program we publish. Our Complete Danjeon Breathing System features a color handbook and six DVDs. We also sell the less expensive exercise DVDs. For this 10-step program we are going to use the clarity exercise featured on our low impact exercise DVD.

The low-impact clarity exercise is easy to do and it is perfect for the 10-step right brain meditation technique I'm going to share with you. You can learn more about this at feelbetterony-ourown.com.

For those of you, who are already practicing meditation, feel free to add elements of this exercise to your present routine.

So, let's get started.

Step one is to schedule a time of day when you can visit nearby park for a peaceful and uninterrupted experience. Be sure to let someone know where you're going and when you'll be back.

Step two. No slavetronics. Leave your tablet, laptop, smart phone, and other handheld devices behind. Turning these devices off so you can take them with you will not work. This is because the mere possession of them will distract you.

Step three. Find a location you like with a strong sensation of life force energy. Ideally, near a tree. Your spot must be surrounded by life force energy, also known as Chi, Ki or Prana.

Step four. You need to ground yourself, so weather permitting, remove your shoes and socks. You need to be barefooted for best results.

Step five. A great way to quickly release negative energy is to hug a tree. Lean into the tree with your body and wrap your arms around it. Send thoughts of love to the tree and ask it to drain away your stresses by grounding you to the Earth.

As you do, imagine the process happening in your mind as the negative energy in your body is drawn out of you by the tree and redirected downward into the ground.

Step six. Once you feel grounded, it is time to prepare for your still state. Thank the tree and find a comfortable place nearby to lie down if you are using the Danjeon Breathing clarity exercise. For other methods, sitting cross-legged on the ground works just as well.

It is okay to use a thin blanket for comfort, as long as you can feel the contour of the ground beneath you.

Step seven. Now you must enter a still state using Danjeon Breathing or any other meditation technique of your choice. In a still state your mind is clear, your body is relaxed and your breathing is steady, comfortable and controlled.

When you reach the last pose of the Danjeon Breathing clarity exercise, you will be in a still state, provided you faithfully follow the exercise instructions.

Remember, this is not a strengthening exercise so never push into pain.

Step eight. Once you have achieved a still state, it is time to experience your surroundings. If you're lying down, slowly change to a cross-legged pose near the tree. It is okay to use a thin blanket as long as you can feel the contour of the ground beneath you. Make sure your breathing is steady and paced and that your mind is clear. Then begin experiencing the world around you with as many of your senses as possible.

It is not important to use all your senses at once, but rather, it is better to explore them sequentially, one at a time. Do not evaluate what your senses detect. Just experience what they do detect as you keep your mind perfectly still.

Everything you've done so far in the first eight steps has prepared you for the most important part of this exercise.

Earlier, I told you about the ancient Polynesians and how they navigated vast distances of the Pacific using a style of right brained navigation that combined free association, synthesizing and holistic thinking to observed the world about them for navigation clues.

During the coming tribulation, a similar right brained approach to survival will help you become more adept at finding water, shelter and sustenance and this is just a mere token of what is possible. So, let's move on to the next step.

With step nine, you will explore the four spheres of the world around you. They are the lithosphere, the ground beneath you, the hydrosphere, all of the surface water on our planet, the biosphere, which is comprised of all life on the planet, and finally, the atmosphere, all of the gases between the lithosphere below us and the fringe of space above us.

Unlike the previous step where you sequentially focused on each of your senses you want to begin experiencing and observing synergistic interactions between the four spheres.

For example, feel the sun on your face. Imagine its warmth working its way down along your body and into the ground beneath you.

Hear the sound of water trickling in a nearby fountain and children at play in the distance.

Smell the scent of flowers in bloom and insects gathering nectar.

This is the most important step in the exercise, so for best results, never begin with expectations.

Likewise, never consciously analyze what you're experiencing. If you do, your left brain will begin to dominate your awareness, causing you to lose the right brain benefits of the experience.

This is essential to building your right brain functions and when you are doing this as you should, something wonderful can happen. From out of nowhere, an epiphany or vision can come to you. It could be a powerful insight into nature or the meaning of something you never saw before. Whatever it is, simply acknowledge it. Again, do not let your left brain steal the show.

And finally, we come to step 10, completion. When you are finished, slowly and methodically gather yourself and your things together and leave. As you return to your home or office, delay thinking about material matters for as long as possible. Rather, use this quality time to contemplate what you've experienced. Relish these impressions like a butterscotch candy slowly dissolving in your mouth.

Speaking of things that are tasty some are very tasty and at the same time very deadly for tribulation survivors.

22

Tribulation Death Foods – Mitigating Their Negative Effects

A tribulation death food is any food that stimulates the growth of harmful yeast and bacteria in your gut. Eat this food and you will become stricken with debilitating bowel issues, lethargy, lack of clarity, and other complaints. Worse of all tribulation death foods will increase the chances of you succumbing to disease.

The reason for this is that 70% of the body's immune system is in the gut, which is why Hippocrates warns us that, "All disease starts in the gut."

Therefore to mitigate the negative effects of tribulation death food, we need to avoid them, and if we cannot, we need to find ways to suppress the growth of candida yeast in our gut and to keep a healthy balance of bacteria.

Even in the best of times and circumstances, we can never eliminate bad bacteria so we do, the next best thing. We manage it. The goal is to maintain a ratio of 80% good bacteria to 20% bad bacteria.

As a teacher, mentor and comforter, you need to impress upon the community leaders that any food that impairs the immune system, is a tribulation death food. For this reason, when stockpiling survival supplies, it is best to avoid highly processed or packaged non-organic foods.

If you must stockpile processed foods, be sure they contain no GMO, pesticides, chemicals, sugar, high fructose corn syrup or artificial sweeteners.

And what about those flavored coffees we enjoy at Starbucks? While there are pros and cons about coffee and health, most flavored coffee drinks contain far more sugar than a can of Coke.

This is important because sugar is the favorite food of bad bacteria in the gut as well as cancer cells. The point being, if you want to enjoy coffee just learn to drink it black and skip the sugar and artificial sweeteners.

For those who wonder why modern foods contain these harmful ingredients, please remember what we learned in the second part of this series, Nibiru Pole Shift – Who Lives, Who Dies, about the agenda of the one percent of the one percent who control our world.

Their goal is to reduce the global population so they can restore their enslavement of our species after the tribulation has passed. Ergo, the harmful ingredients their corporations put into our food are setting us up to fail during the tribulation.

Consequently stockpiling the best possible foods for survival will be difficult and expensive. However, there is a way to mitigate the negative effects with a probiotic strategy.

There are essentially two probiotic options: supplemental and natural.

A good thing to stockpile for the tribulation will be probiotic supplements. When shopping for supplements, there are three things to look for when evaluating competitive formulations:

Seven or more unique strains of gut-friendly bacteria is one. Make sure they are acid and bile resistance. This is necessary so they can get the good bacteria to where it is needed.

And be mindful of the CF use value colony forming units. In general, the more the better.

I firmly believe that probiotics are a stockpiling must for the tribulation so please do not rush into this, as the cost of these supplements varies widely, and paying more does not necessarily mean you'll get more. This is why I strongly urge you to take the time to thoroughly research this topic so that you can make an informed buying decision on your own and please be sure to shop with merchants you already know and trust.

In addition to probiotic supplements you should also incorporate natural probiotics into your stockpiling plans as well.

Excellent sources are pickled and fermented foods and at the top of the list is a Korean favorite, Kimchi. Made from salted and fermented vegetables such as cabbage and radishes, it is a powerful probiotic and one you can learn to make yourself.

Another is Kombucha, an ancient Chinese fermented sweetened tea drink you can brew at home. While you can find it in the store, I prefer to brew it myself. Amongst its many benefits is that it is a great way to fight candida because it contains live probiotic cultures.

As with probiotic supplements, I strongly urge you to learn about natural probiotics and how to make them yourself. Then start making them today so that you'll know exactly what to do.

During the tribulation when it comes to stockpiling here is the bottom line. The one percent of the one percent who control the world from the shadows want us to die in vast numbers. It is why their food corporations are setting us up to fail during the tribulation and why it is virtually impossible to defend ourselves against this without breaking the bank. But with a strong probiotic strategy, you can mitigate enough of this damage to make a real difference.

There is also another thing you can do to mitigate the negative effects of harmful ingredients to our gut. It's called Danjeon Breathing.

It does not require a formulation or a food. It is an ancient Korean self-healing energy art that traces its roots back to the early days of acupuncture. It is widely practiced in Korea and is slowly becoming popular in America.

Most who study Danjeon Breathing in America come from other disciplines such as yoga and Reiki and are very advanced in their practice. They study and adopt Danjeon Breathing so they can include it within their existing health and wellness regimes.

The remainder of those who begin the practice of Danjeon Breathing in America do it for low back pain. Given the gentle method of this art, it is highly effective in helping low back pain sufferers.

In my own case, I began the practice of Danjeon Breathing because I was stricken with a very severe case of irritable bowel syndrome, IBS, a problem that will be sure to haunt tribulation survivors.

After two weeks, I was symptom free after doing Danjeon Breathing for just 20 minutes each day. After three months, I was completely healed and I was free to eat whatever I liked. To learn more about Danjeon Breathing, visit feelbetteronyourown.com.

And now, one final thought on natural remedies before we move on.

When you begin researching this and other natural solutions on the Internet, you are going to find a lot of misleading and disparaging information such as articles telling you that these natural solutions are not good for you because their benefits have not been proved or that they are actually dangerous.

Before you give these attacks the benefit of the doubt, please understand one simple point. While there are those who believe they're being honest and through integrity, put their names and faces before the public, there are many more who are far less forthcoming. In fact, the more you try to learn about them, the less you come to know about them and their true agendas.

This is how the majority of negative attacks are spread across the Internet by paid disinformationalists. Elusive people with multiple paper thin personas.

Before you put your life and the lives of those you love in the hands of such people, think about it because there is only one person who truly deserves the benefit of the doubt – you and you alone.

Now that we've added mind and body tools to our Perpetual Genesis toolbox it's time to take a soulful look at your role in the coming tribulation.

.

23

Be a Helping Hand – Share Hope for the Future with Other

After months if not years into the tribulation, there will come the darkest of days, when it will not matter how well-equipped or well provisioned you are because during these dark days, you will lurch from one crisis to the next with an unending sense of suffering and an absence of hope for the future. It will be in these dark days when some lay their heads down to sleep at night and pray "Dear God I am so weary of this world. Please take me in my sleep."

If they've led good lives and are worthy, God may answer their prayers. If not, it will mean they have something more to learn in this life and they will awaken to another day of tribulation. But if they are fortunate, you as a sensitive with the ability to see others holistically will understand their pain.

This is when you will sit beside them and gently place a helping hand upon their shoulder. Then you will softly say "how is your world today?"

When they talk, you will listen respectfully, and when they ask, "What's the point of carrying on?" you will pause for a brief moment before answering as you turn to look them directly in the eyes. When you see them searching your eyes for compassion and insight is the moment when you will share with them a message of hope for the future.

It must be neither glib nor extemporaneous. Rather, what you will share with them will be your vision of a better life. One that helps you to carry on as well.

It is why those who join our church create this vision in their own mission victory plan or MVP for short. The MVP is the first tool. Our members add to their Perpetual Genesis survival toolkit and it begins with a vision of success on the backside a time beyond the tribulation years. When we see blue skies and taste sweet waters once again.

This is a vision so you do not tell it with words. Rather, you show it with words with what we call IMAX clarity. This will be the vision you share with that sad soul facing another dark day, and whose prayer for the relief from life went unanswered.

You must become a helping hand in the community, if you are to succeed as a teacher, mentor and comforter. You must be seen by one and all as much more than the eyes and ears of the leadership.

Yes. When leaders look up, they need to see the print of your helping hand everywhere in the community but the same is true for the community members as well. They need to must see the prints of your helping hand everywhere.

It is why your helping hand strategy needs to be simple. If you focus all of your efforts on the needs of just a few to the exclusion of the many, you will not be seen as a helping hand. Rather, you may come to be seen as an emotional crutch that can be ill afforded by a community hard-pressed by the daily business of tribulation survival.

On the other hand, if you devote yourself to being a helping hand for as many as you can each day, then you will become valuable.

Your job will be those brief caring moments when you let others know that they are not alone. Not to commiserate over irreconcilable griefs and complaints.

Rather, seek those eager to learn new skills of value to the community if given the right kind of help. When you do, then find others in the community capable and willing to be of service to them and introduce them together, with that very purpose in mind. In the process the sharing of useful self-sufficiency knowledge will help each of them to feel greater hope for the future.

This is what it means to be a helping hand.

To learn more read my book *Survival Wellness Advocacy and the Big WIN*. Print editions are available for purchase. But the e-book version is free our web site at knowledgemountain.org.

We hope you'll use the information in this book to see if our strategy for surviving the tribulation appeals to you.

We've covered a lot of ground in this three-part series, and so now I want to leave you with the most important thing to remember if you only remember one thing.

This is that one thing to remember.

Surviving the coming Planet X tribulation is not about holding onto things. It is about holding on to each other, and I'll leave it on that note.

So until the next time we meet, remember Marshall's motto. Destiny comes to those who listen, and fate finds the rest. So learn what you can learn, do what you can do, and never give up hope. For the knowledge Mountain Church of Perpetual Genesis, I'm Marshall Masters.

ANNOUNCER: This program was made possible by the Knowledge Mountain Church of Perpetual Genesis. To learn more visit knowledgemountain.org. We also encourage you to pursue your awareness path by reading Marshall's book, *Surviving the Planet X Tribulation: A Faith-Based Leadership Guide*. To learn more, visit planetxtribulation.com. This concludes this three-part series.

Alphabetical Index

Made in the USA
Monee, IL
03 July 2023

38601731R00066